BEWARE
THE
HOUSE

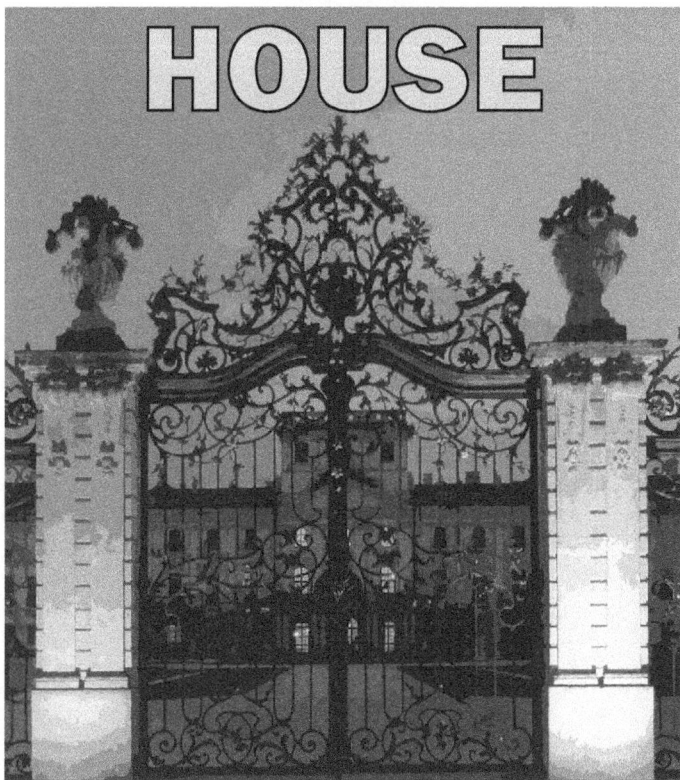

POEMS BY
SUSANNA RICH

The Poet's Press
PITTSBURGH, PA

www.poetspress.org

ISBN 978-0-922558-34-6
This is the 239th publication of The Poet's Press
Also published in Adobe Acrobat (PDF) format.

THE POET'S PRESS
2209 Murray Avenue #3
Pittsburgh, PA 15217-2338

TABLE OF CONTENTS

VII. DOLL HOUSE

EPILOGUE: HAUNTED HOUSE

Art — a House that tries to be haunted.
— Emily Dickinson

PROLOGUE

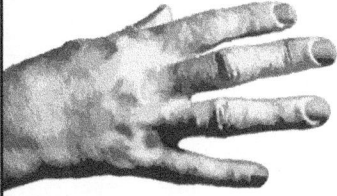

OPEN HOUSE

BEWARE THE HOUSE WITH NO CORNERS —

the round house, like a massive breast
suctioned to a knoll;
like the eyes and skull of a buried giant.

Enter this cyclotron to braille the inner wall,
never to know where you entered
or if you can leave.

Wings are embedded in the broken china floors,
wooden fish gossip in the inverted bowl of air
breathing itself like a sponge.

Nothing meets itself. No right angles
corner spirits. And don't ask doors to shut
or open in jambs meant not to true.

An orange paper jellyfish hangs,
clitoral, at the center,
to vacuum you into the glass dome.

Sling your quilt over your head
to spiral on Escher stairs —
wander your sleep among distant thumps

and whistling goats.
This mandala is all a basement
and attic, with no between.

Ghosts loll their tongues, thick as boots;
ride you like a zebra,
as the calliope plays.

<13>

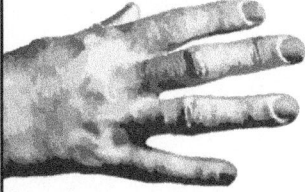

I

MY
HOUSE

possession;

dream edge of my body,
and Mummy, here,
to scoop out my eyes,

press them, like violets,
into her book;
she screws off my ears

to dry in her oven —
conchs of sounds
I hear for her;

for the savor of words,
a swallow of truth,
she carves out my mouth —

plants my teeth
under her pillow
to grow her tomorrow's eyes,

shell ears, wing mouth;
and I, here,
sleep myself hard

as if I weren't the one
taking

<17>

The Buck

When I am six years old,
Grandmother tells me to
get her stuffed when she dies —
like the front door buck head,
catching webs of evil
between six-point antlers.

The living room, of course,
is where we're to seat her —
on the sofa (or chair),
behind the piano
where I will play Chopin,
Brahms, Schumann, Beethoven.

And sew her eyes open
(maybe a touch of glass),
looking up to the right —
like sweet Saint Theresa,
clasping her red roses;
or holey Sebastian.

Her hands are to be sheathed —
white lace fingerless gloves —
propped wide for heaven's bowl;
her lips slightly parted
to show her pearly teeth —
her mouth channeling God.

<18>

Never to be alone —
while I shop for perfume
or oil for her skin,
or a bulb for her lamp —
she and the buck will wait
for my timely return.

Times and times my six years,
I bang at my keyboards
 — webs worry my eyes, mouth,
my hands, my many pores —
shadow antlers quiver
fingers across my scores.

<19>

Grandmother Sausages

She strokes the salty lamb guts
onto her finger like a long blue
stocking into a wrinkle of rings

and pulls them inside out to stretch
onto the maw of the grinder
screwed to the metal-edged table

I turn the crank   She presses
her *nothing cuts* into the well
Chicken hearts and thighs   she says

You Grandfahder hand   no be
Liberace   no rings   no glass
pianos   no chandelier

no money   no hope
Pig things grinding   she says
You Fahder arm   no be   Victor Mature

pushèd de column
loving hees Delilah
Heem sit   scratch   pick nose roll

und me me must to be my own butcher
Brains   kidneys   tongues
I could to sing Salome

to de Luhvrence Velk
could to be Phyllis Diller
but no   you Uncle crazy head

<20>

and her first love's *nevers*
and her father's *nos*   Crank
crank crank   necks   snouts and

shall we call them *tails*
worming through the grinder
like words through a telephone

When all the guts are stuffed
the way   Grandmother says
they force-feed geese to fatten their livers

we tie off and twist meat braids
for Grandfather's smokehouse to cure
His eaves are so well hung

with salamis   kielbasas   head cheese
that I climb up to dangle my legs
among the blood links for her

to dance her fingers along
as if among chimes
and sing   Grandmama   sing sing

<21>

Daddy, First Communion Sunday, Lassie

You needed to yourself
This child newly blessed

    Lassie was on your hot new set,
    leaping over a fence.

I   crumpled on your belly
You   on your back

    Jeff had no Daddy —
    that's why they gave *him* Lassie.

You rocked and rocked us on your bed
You *Wowed* your *Wows*

    Lassie was going blind.
    Doc Weaver had no hope.

The Virgin Mary on the wall I faced
Held one finger up   in warning

    Jeff walked all the way to the vet in Capitol City,
    even offered his own eye for Lassie.

Or was Mother Mary pointing
to someone in Heaven
To bless the child sitting on her thigh

    Someone was always leaving a child on *Lassie* —
    for a fire, for grandma, for forever.

Press   press you said   wanting me
To be stronger   sometimes

<22>

And then, when the child was alone,
out of the woods would come the lion or the bear

You   pressing against my hands
Was I in my white gown and veil good enough

Timmy was an orphan and a runaway.
Lassie found *him* in the barn.

You in your torn socks   had lifted me
Onto your lap for the test

Gramps died. Timmy almost drowned.
Lassie saved him.

Was I who had Jesus the Savior in my belly strong enough
You yanked my shoulders to pull me down

Jeff and his Mom left the farm. Lassie stayed
with Timmy and his new dad and mom.

Mommy would not come back to you no matter how I tried
You said you were my *Lassie* and to ride you like a pony

Timmy knelt to say "Now I lay me down."
Lassie put her front paws on the bed next to him, praying.

<23>

My Mother's Kitchen is Her Pontiac,

and her favorite recipe is

Road Kill Deer

Jacklight: 1 buck in your high beams
Truss: 1 chop to the manifold
Drive hard to roast deep.
Serve: No one.

My mother's Tempest features Blue Hubcap specials:
Weed and Rush Salad with Gravel Croutons,
Road-Splash Shake, and (my personal favorite)
Mirage Soufflé du Pot Hole. I know —

I'm her bobble-headed waitress on the back shelf:
the *Hey Doll!* in a wide crocheted dress,
legs anchored in the empty core of a toilet paper roll,
arms holding an invisible order pad and pen.

My mother feeds me glances
in her rearview mirror —
all she can spare from gunning the engine,
dodging radar, steering into lights.

Behind us, tracks bruise the road,
like footsteps do flour in some childhood
kitchen, where ovens make sleep, knives
blood, and from boiling water hands wave.

Beyond the *no-no, no-no* of her wipers
lies the poppy-seed road with banana yellow lines.
She cuts her wheels along them as if to slash
the fugitive ground, gut it of its ashes and mines.

<24>

The road unrolls; the tank runs dry.
She leans back into her seat, torn from shifting weight;
burns a wad of its stuffing in the cigarette lighter;
passes it back to me as toast.

No matter. I can stop shaking my head
off its spring. I can stop waiting.
I am the one with the invisible pen,
and the necessary papers under her skirts.

<25>

Playgirl

Like Loco Jones on *How to Marry a Millionaire*,
my choosy Susie mother was always learning
how to bag a millionaire father for me.
That's why, I supposed, she stashed *Playboys* and *Penthouses*
under the red skirts of the studio couch
where (if she was home) she slept.

All that needing-a-father she said I had
was why I had to be alone at nights,
and why, while refilling my Cross fountain pen,
I dropped the empty permanent blue ink cartridge,
and, patting around for it, found her slick cache.

I knew it was wrong, but I figured if I were *bad* enough,
she'd come home to catch me.
So I thumbed open the centerfolds,
lay them around me into a wagon train —
a witches' circle of heads to butts, to heads to butts:

here was Miss April wearing nothing but
long black leather boots and elbow gloves,
touching herself with a whip;
and Miss Yes-You-May in a crawl-away pose,
rump arched, red as a baboon's;

and Miss Cherry June, her long, long tongue
licking (actually stuck to) the popsicle of her finger,
as if it didn't belong to her.
Fireworks July, Hurricane August —
all those misses of the month — their parts bare;
lips pursed, or puckered, or open — yet not.

<26>

And balloons and balloons of bosoms pressed together
like babies' butts (into cracks), nipples hard-pointing
at me, and me looking back, and touching them —
yet not. If only I could have taught my mother
what I learned from Miss Ding-a-Ling School Belle
September, Miss *Hello Weenie* October, and the
Spanksgiving Twins — as we held and held and held
and held our difficult poses — but together:
that wanting alone, and making-believe
won't hustle love home.

<27>

I Am the Snake Milker's Daughter,

standing outside the serpentarium window,
   watching my father's captive asps,
      mambas, vipers —
       coiling, recoiling in their vivariums:
    they who are always longer
   than wide, limbless enough to slither.
They greet him, as he comes through the door —
   tongues tasting his musk,
         rattlers in chorus,
        symphony of sizzles —
   buzzing their circumscribed glass.
   He unhooks a screen cover.
The taipan sidles to the far corner.
         She's the fullest.
         She must come first.
    My father loops her head
     in the triangular pin stick, hoists her
      onto the metal podium,
    under the funnel suspended
   under a vial. He pinches her head,
winds her body around his arm. Her fangs
   penetrate the rubber membrane stretched
     over the mouth of the vial.
      The drip of yellow venom.
     The cucumber smell of fear.
   The serums, antivenins.
The hearts they will save.
     I play my flute — my *pungi*, my *been*. I play
      for my father. For Cleopatra and Eve.
       For the times my father was bitten.

<28>

Never Was a Wolf

Little, little me,
bigger will I be —
like lungs boiling in the pot —
I'm going to burst free.
　— Hungarian children's rhyme

Grandmother double-bubbled
pink calf lungs in frothing pots,
plopped in wide-eyed cuts of marrow bone,
Slinky chicken necks, pigs' knuckle balls.

The lid sputtered and drummed,
marrows oozed, bones melted,
lungs swelled gray over the rim —
then gurgled into my bowl.

My picture-book animals oinked,
screamed, lowed inside my belly
 — their lungs became my lungs,
their weakened bones my hard —

as Grandmother pressed her fingers
into my mouth to make me
suck away her grease, so that
one day, while she cooed over me

about my wet tongue and sweet lips,
how she could eat me up, my lungs
would swell, I'd bite her hard and free.

<29>

A Baby Sister

Bloody towel
Mummy
holds between her legs,
the little sister she won't
have for me — I cut
paper dolls
with no eyes, no mouths, no hands
reaching through no hands; hang
mirrors facing mirrors;
place doll chairs
next to adult;
lay scissors
under my
pillow,
in case
I'm next.

<30>

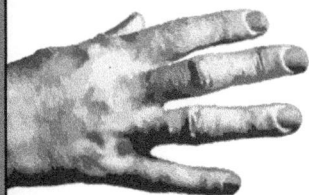

THE HOUSE

Requiem for a Terrorist's Hands

All flesh shall come before Thee.
                              — Verdi's *Requiem*

Devotion bent — did those hands know —
one on the throttle, the other on the yoke?

Dirt half-moon nails, river palms —
when the damned are cast away

and consigned to searing flame —
did the fingers curl to boast their clutch?

Did they rise to bless their own *salaam*?
Banking left, banking right —

did they sever free of the pilot who only steers?
My blind knuckles scallop my steering wheel.

May those other hands have known, again,
their *mudra*s of fin, hoof, wing.

The engine spits its fires — gears bite gears.
How perfect the love of our bodies.

<33>

Adopt-a-Corpse —

Is your life a Sham-Wow?
Are you a war-stats junkie —
a numbers-jockeying newshead?
Then Oxyclean with Adopt-a-Corpse!

Nothing down — it's yours!
Take this child torched in a crawl-away pose!
Or this man, face clearing
under a cinderblock wall,

his body on the other side
dissolved to a nuclear ooze!
Someone is waiting for you —
chin dropped, lips curled back,

chanting maggots and worms.
Mighty Putty your corpse
in the lower left of your dreams
to caption your acquisitions and lusts.

(Warning: you may get lice, boils,
and depressed; you may lose heart;
your pressure might go up;
you might faint; you might die...)

But *it* will need no pajamas!
No sunny-side ups! No glasses of milk!
Only let it lose its life
more fully in yours.

<34>

Call toll-free, while supplies last.
And in the next 10, 9, 8...
we'll include three land mines
and a packet of anthrax

for DIY.
Hurry! Be quick!
Choose. Before you are
Kaboom!

<35>

From a Mother in the Garden of Grief

— Inspired by Suse Lowenstein's sculpture, *Dark Elegy*,
for the victims of the terrorist bombing of Pan Am Flight 103
over Lockerbie, Scotland, December 21, 1988

Among scatters of fingernail, button,
watch, our hands swell into branches,
breasts spread into canopies,

toes like rows of fat teeth root earth.
In asanas of welded pain,
we rub our bodies with shards of steel,

ground glass, and ash,
to numb ourselves into stone angels or crows.
We pour, like lava, over what is left,

as if we could
mold a shoelace into a vein,
an earring into an ovary,

a torn sock into a heart. Turn,
we turn, as if we could unspin
eons, decompose into water

and salt, and start over —
learn again how to have eyes,
how to lift our heads,

<36>

how to split open like seeds
        from the strains of gravity
      and fire,

          from the having to look
          so grief won't
          grow.

<37>

Puddling: Two Weeks After 9/11

*Puddling: the male butterfly drinking
contaminated water, sweat, urine, or
excreta for salt to shore up his libido.*

*Puddling: Purification of impure metal by
heating and stirring.*

1
Union Beach, across New York Bay,
I explain to the Havens Grill hostess:
I need soup, and, Archie, a spoon
of apple juice. Since business

is *slow*, as she puts it, I can, she says,
stay — table for one — brings me no
menu, yesterday's luke bisque,
saltines she rustles from her pocket —

not-looking at Archie, my monarch
butterfly poised between the smiling
lips of the blue plastic airplane
sand-molding toy I found

on the post-storm beach among
rust-headed flicked-out Bics;
remnants of treaded mouths of
unidentifiable plastic containers;

and a white Shaker sweater, stilled
mid-writhe — thrown? wrested?
— lost, in any case,
with its pack of swollen Camels.

<38>

2

Four thin black butterfly legs flailed where
the surf stroked the wings it was burying —
there, the squirm and its sand-foundered
orange and black wedge — the something I could

spirit to a half scudder shell
on a mini-butte of reddish sand —
scoop water with the plastic airplane
(I wouldn't otherwise have handled),

pour grit off all that shuddering;
pry, to release, with a pen cap,
the tamped tissue of wings,
their talc too gone for flight.

<39>

3

Havens Grill, grateful for hands encumbered
by these gifts of the surf, I couldn't unscramble
the hair across my face, unskew
my glasses spotted with salt spray.

So I earned the right to *something* —
ease of anonymity, perhaps. Perhaps
I wanted to be marked *homeless* — be part
of the greater belonging. So why

explain (as if explaining does)
to the woman who once-overed
my fishy sweater, or the meter
person who waxed too passionate

with ticket-writing to look up.
They would not understand
why I was *hah*ing my breath
into the blue lips of a plastic airplane

to warm a butterfly and its orange stained-glass
weight, its whip tongue coiled
hard into its mouth.

<40>

4

He clung to my finger,
thorny legs clasped
to faults in my skin —

this creature almost drowned
in the salt water it puddled
to shore up for mating.

I wanted to believe it was
over a chasm deeper than species
that he clung and clung, although

I offered him goldenrod after goldenrod,
down the line of dunes
I walked — a figure as comical

as anyone might need —
bowing to flowers,
whispering ...

<41>

5

My '02 Avalon and its installments,
my cells and laminations were parked
miles and a morning away —

how little it took to slough off the shell
of solitary-mid-life-traveler —
unprepared for sudden cold

— to enter the realm — breath to breath —
of a butterfly and the sound, as if
of my own eyelids, fluttering.

6

After our Havens lunch, I take Archie
to a butterfly bush filled
with identical guests
(but for the tear in his hind wing).

The spring of his proboscis
unfurls into a blossom. He anchors
his legs, pulses with drinking,
then rises, grasping for air,

like a hand learning to wave.
When I drive back later, I find
his body gutted, a neighbor explains,
by a praying mantis.

<42>

7

Who can anticipate the gates
grief fashions for itself or how its

freedoms might appear?
Engine idling, strapped, again, into

my multi-adjustable power bucket seat,
I hold vigil outside a shuttered beach house.

There, a woman as substantial as last August,
takes a make-believe shower — mimes the pour

of shampoo from an invisible bottle; fingers veils
of no-water through her auburn hair to spread

across her shoulders; saw-saws a missing towel
pressing, almost, like wings into her back.

<43>

Piñata

The piñata is the emblem of Las Posadas,
a winter solstice commemoration
of the stable where, coming to destroy
treachery and vice, evil and darkness,
the Son of David brought light.

Because the newly-elected one is a suit
(devoted to cover-ups),
with a red tie, like an old lion drooling blood —
we hang him from a string —

a papier-maché voodoo piñata —
in the back yard behind the fence
(where no one can report us),
from a clothing rack on wheels, of course.

At first, we blindfold each other —
to represent the faith of voters
convinced of justice, then spin each other
around — as that is what has happened

to us all. We take turns: *whack* a wooden spoon
at this made-to-order effigy from Mexico.
Unbudging surfaces, it swings (no surprise)
and dodges. We find a broomstick, for magic,

and aim for the seven deadlies —
attack the crêpe-y, creepy mouth,
for its unsatiable *Gula; thwack* the groin
for his pussy-grabbing *Fornicatio;*

<44>

whack the corseted paunch for bragging *Superbia*;
crack his fingers for blame-pointing *Ira*.
We *hack* at the no-hole *Vanagloria* ears,
smack his poor-me *Tristitia* jowls, but

nothing gives. Not even *knocking* at the butt
fattened by *Avaritia* and lazy *Acedia*.
It grins and gloats. Then David, last to try,
hits the one place hollow enough —

the heart.

<45>

The Trees Are Falling Because They Must

I see a branch of the watchful tree (Jeremiah 1:11-12).

New Haven green: The Lincoln Oak heaves up
a human skull, jaws agape among exposed roots.
And elms *kamikaze* onto the Bronco, the Matrix —
the Jag glutted with Exxon, Sunoco, Shell.

The trees are doing what they can:
fan-leafed gingkoes faint onto garages;
poplars *yee-hah* onto Sertas,
axe Maytags, scrape Vizios off walls.

That kettle-drumming is the fall of spruce trees
scoring streets into musical staffs —
loosening wires to coil and recoil into clefs,
to pizzicato like rattlers.

Colonnades of cypress explode gas lines
and bonzo into the resulting fires.
Maples, like massive pick-up sticks,
rubble trains, logjam rivers, karate bridges.

Of course, yews slam into their own shadows.
Of course, dogwoods release the August sky
to make massive snowballs of themselves,
while willows amputate their own limbs.

Let the beeches ooze their trunks around benches,
Harleys, hydrants, and wrought iron fences.
Appease the teaks reclaiming themselves from chairs;
the pines from paneling; the cedars from pencils.

<46>

Oh, Berkeley, the laurels are hearing each other
fall in forests — the telephone poles are in caucus.
And the sycamore in charge has angled itself,
like a cannon, atop a Dodge Avenger

whose front left Firestone is stalled
on a felled Seventh Day billboard,
on words I thought that I shall never see:
...pare for the Unexpected.

<47>

Abandoned House: Old Mine Road

Right of eminent domain ... your own good —
the river must be dammed for the reservoir
of the future; houses with a view, emptied.

She stood the broom against the wall of the porch,
its handle, like a sundial leaned against the house —
straw bristles anchored between floor slats

to hold the shaft erect as the head withered down —
a witch's talisman against the armed soldiers
who came to evict the hold-outs.

Twenty years have halved her fifteen-light door
into a Dutch gate, bottom flat on the ground,
upper dangling from a locked hasp, knob floating.

What remains? The strew of pink plastic curlers
nestled in brown oak leaves and acorns
by the open oven door. When they came,

did she run into the kitchen to rip the tiny cages
from her hair, as if beauty could save her?
Why wouldn't they let her pick them up?

By the pot belly stove in the living room,
I find a red wooden love-seat, slats half torn up —
and drag it, furtive, out of the house,

shove it into the wide body of my transport.
Before I leave, I turn around and see
her white curtains, waving.

<48>

We're Fringed —

everything is — from our Samson heads to fronded palms.
And what is foot if not sole splaying toes with toenail eyes?
Those ramparts, teeth, are mouth picketing *smooth pink gums* —
and words are a macramé of repetition and resolve.

Something about mobility, then, and flux,
this fugue of what's core, what's not.
We comb, strum, combine; rice, furrow, tread —
cogs hooking cogs; crowds of crosswalk legs.

Fringe is reach and change —
the automatic car wash hula-ing at streaks.
Awnings and dawnings; fencing, flame,
and fork are our necessary serrations

to zipper to each other by. All crenelations
and stripes, the steel fur that is our cities,
the trail of jets, the rotor blades,
the afghan slipping from our laps —

<49>

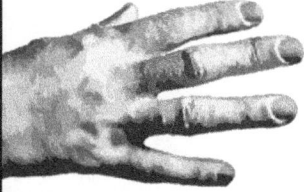

SCHOOL
HOUSE

Ribbons

Blue polka-dot hair band tamed me for Holy Week,
red moiré pigtail streamers on Pentecost,
pink velvet bows at my temples — All Saints'.

Black-wimpled Sister Mathilda, face scored red
by her starched corduroy frame;
Father McLaughlin, tracing orange curls at his throat,

look up — she from slamming Richard Guidelli's head
against the blackboard, he from behind musty curtains —
to mingle their fingers in my Maypole of colors.

Not. They added *No Ribbons* to the St. Nicholas R.C. School
"Code of Conduct" — right before patent leather shoes
reflecting petti-pants, and boys wriggling in their seats.

Grosgrain and satins fray —
despite their ends cut into slants and V's.
They stain, knot, unmatch; wrinkle,

though wet, ironed, hung by color on nails
in the closet I painted red with yellow flowers.
Sister Mathilda's *hallelujah*s become Alzheimer rants;

Father McLaughlin's *Love of God* translated
into two children, divorce, diabetes.
My Christmas Glee Club tinsel crown lies

tarnished and tangled among my ribbons,
in a basement, in a Food Fair plastic bag
rubbed opaque and crazed.

<53>

"School Uniform"

After artist Julie Harris's Howe Gallery installation

Hung on a hook, back cell of the University Gallery —
on a green plastic hanger, two geese carved
in silhouette at its neck —
the blue Catholic school jumper
Julie's mother saved; the white blouse,
collar with rounded lobes, like nippleless breasts.

At St. Nicholas Irish Catholic School
the rich kids wore a Kelly green jumper
too expensive for me; and my mother, who slept
with her divorce lawyer, to free herself
from my Hungarian father who drank,
who beat her when she was pregnant with me.

Into the installation bodice, Julie sewed a photo *intaglio*
of a girl in her First Communion dress,
flowers on her head, her eyes marble blank,
her hand holding up a stick,
like a prosthetic arm.

By Principal Sister Catherine's *imprimatur*,
I wore the Joyce Leslie clearance vest and skirt,
with the black and red windowpane pattern
of the only green outfit they had —
too big and then too small for me —
the Henley tee underneath, safety pin for a button.

In the front of Julie's skirt, where an apron might be,
an iridescent blue ribbon square frames
some torture device — a larva or a wasp's nest,
a chrysalis rayed with sharp spikes.

<54>

What Father Molloy grasped behind
the dark confessional pleats —
the hand I didn't have to hold up
to make him stop — the stick
to draw the curtains aside.
Julie's short sleeves are edged,
as if with two crowns of thorns.

Class 4B with Sister Matilda,
I was ashamed of having to pee, that it was
"down there," that I felt something
that I held and held until I couldn't anymore —
sitting in my school desk
not able to raise my hand to leave,
my Joyce Leslie skirt spongy, dripping, hot.

How perfect, Julie's pleats!
How her gabardine shines
under these gallery lights!.

<55>

Anchor

Father Malloy was the mean priest —
his confessional window a nightmare television
that talked back; black-rimmed coke-bottle glasses,

like binoculars boring into our backs.
Father Malloy filled the doorway of class 7A,
the day the president was shot in the sun —

midnight-blue Lincoln convertible,
pretty Jackie in her pink suit, pink pillbox hat;
the red roses they gave her at Love Field, Texas.

Father Malloy trooped us to church,
as if we were, somehow, to fault —
right hand clamped on Dennis Resnick's neck,

the other waving like Death's scythe —
his hard-set jaws willing our slow march,
our sobs echoing up the walls. Early dismissal,

we went home to Walter Cronkite waiting for us
in our Zeniths and Motorolas. Replay after replay,
we watched him look up at his clock,

take off his glasses, and announce —
President Kennedy died at 1:00 PM,
2:00 PM Eastern Standard Time.

<56>

His chin cramped up.
Throat swallowing hard.
Not to weep, himself, Walter Cronkite
steadied us with his eyes after Jackie
kissed the flag-draped coffin,
and John-John saluted.

His voice carried us
through the riderless black horse,
the bullets' angles —
making us feel that, in him,
we still had a father;
that, next time, we would know

to put a bubble over the limo,
to not go to Love Field,
to not wear pink.

His was the face that always returned
and stayed between us
and *whatever* happened.

Some nights, I turned the volume down,
and confessed all my miserable little sins
to Walter Cronkite in his box of light.

He lip-synced my words, (exactly
as I said them) and we always ended
with *That's the way it is. That's the way...*

<57>

Fly in Our Classroom:
While Reading the Death Scene
from *Romeo and Juliet*

Ducking — you are — leaning
in your one-armed seats, as if riding Harleys
or wheelchair dancing —

squealing at the uninvited,
the many-armed, the small enough
to fit anywhere, and free.

You look to me as if I, with perfect aim,
could slam my book on unpredictability,
nurse you through all

that's disturbing or strange.
I disappoint you, as I must, in this, and all:
I have no words to fix love or death —

to make one stay, the other leave.
What can I do, but spin the loose light switch
so we can stop resisting the dark?

I open the door to let this fly —
buzzing spawn of air, vent, and
fluorescent tubes — seek light

in the corridor. Let us return, then,
to this shared room of our lives —
our writhing hands, our multiple hungry eyes.

<58>

Gargoyles

Masters of the high gutter —
troughs in their backs
to channel roof water
through their gargling throats,
past façades of friable mortar, stone.

Grotesques we call the winged dragon
hurling, the flying monkey frozen
mid-flight, the ghoul with lizard tongue;
nose-pickers, half-frog faces — eyes
fixed, mouth gaping — conduits, all —

as are Gargoogling students in halls,
or undergrounders texting on platforms,
or workers surfing by the garage elevator —
backs buttressing cinderblock walls;
legs angled into number 4s.

Fingers claw-like, thumbs brailling,
they cradle their third hands,
their spouts of ethereal spew —
garble from The Cloud, Facebook feed —
gorgonized, gaga, agog.

<59>

Wolfbank Grades

A

My Ms. Goody Goody student and your seatedness,
Papermate erect for my entering
the room — come take your full 40%
participation for your eagerness
to guess what I'm thinking,
to scribble my every aside —

and 60% for your laser printed, clipped
(not stapled), MLA documented, page-more-than-required
papers and the regulation thank-you Ecard
and my gratitude for this ease, this not having to justify
your forgettability.

A-

10% out of 40% participation lost
for all the 20 minutes late —
the sloshing through others' books and shoes
for the front row seat — unsnap-snapping your briefcase,
unvelcro-ing your coat — capping and uncapping
your highlighter through the best of
"Prufrock," "Lady Lazarus,"
"Because I could not stop for Death."

58% for questions I couldn't answer
that you did, for tossing me your sheaf of fourth grade
poems filled with the luxury of brilliance,
unencumbered with Academic Standards,
tenure lunches, politically correct
Released Time projects and envy —
or the fear of it.

<60>

B+

for your three children, crisp suit, pocked iPhone case
the slow safe, plodding report
of everyone else's literary criticism —
the office visits, stylishly brief.
I add your expected plus —
noblesse largesse from me.

B

You are less likely to grieve, less
likely to laugh at my balding,
or say I'm too old or too indifferent,
less likely to hate poetry as you would
for a B-.

C

Binder full of plastic-sleeved pages
desktop-published by your father's secretary,
her Marlboro smoke wafting as I open
your cover: your lacrosse career,
your place in the family.

C

because the Union wouldn't pass C- or D++
for the likes of you layering on another film
of mousse or gel to the brown fog etched
by heads across the painted cinderblock wall —
lady of the black claws with diamond crescents,
life manicured for diner tips,
that fourteen carat breastplate of chains,
those lips too moistly violet for words.

<61>

D

Fail you? Make you eligible to retake this course?
Give you a forum with a wisp instructor
and her round knowings — firm young morals —
whom you'd tell how I assigned papers
on your body parts, your most unspeakable wants —
to take the risks that poets risk —
saying what mustn't-be-said?

F

Phantom of 101, my plagiarist, my quick-escapéd worm —
you are the non-you I want to multiply and register
in alphabetic lines — to hear the clattering
of your non-existent boots against the chairs
as I toss — to your silent applause —
all your non-papers and non-exams,
your poetic aspirations down the Well of Grades.

<62>

Multiple Seed:
To Students Writing Poetry
in Response to Williams' *Paterson*

You start by writing Hallmark cards —

> I will love you eternally.
> You always made my day.
> You were always there for me.
> Please don't go away.

You see, you say, *It could be*
about your town, your mother —
even poetry. Readers can guess.

Packets of seeds hibernate in my refrigerator
with gauze sachets of dried milk absorbing moisture.
Shall I pour them all — carrots, beets, lettuce,
cosmos, forget-me-nots — into one dibbled hole?
Flood them with all the water they'll ever need?
Pile on a yard of chicken manure,
a congress of beneficial nematodes?
Shall I then tell my garden, as I flourish my hoe —
Work it out for yourselves?

I know the yearning for the paradisiac *it*
of being sought and understood without pains.
But, as Williams said, *The local is the only universal.*
Poetry is in the kneeling and the getting dirty;
in the learning to weed — and to wait.

<63>

Combing Through *Hamlet*

Sarah-Elisabeth (a.k.a. "Harley") is cornered
in the Formica embrace of her school desk, last row,
walls flanking her raised elbows —
chestnut hair dyed Viking saffron,
streaked with DayGlo bubblegum pink.

Fortinbras is a War Machine, she says,
plaiting the right side of her hair
into a wispy-ended warrior's plait —
hooked fingers left/right punching
— and ties off with a Goody Ponytail rubber band.

The queen's only problem is she's jealous of Ophelia,
Harley says, swirling and knotting her left locks
onto the top of her head, ends fanning like a half tiara.
She wedges a hairpin tip behind her front teeth,
pries it open, and says,

Illusion — always illusion in Hamlet.
Harley tugs the elastic off her braid,
twists the crimped tresses until they inscribe
tight enraveled rolls, like the *fallera*
ringing Princess Leia's ears.

Ophelia is lying to him, Harley says,
and yanks out her braids and twistings,
shakes her hair out into a staticky halo.
When Laertes jumps into Ophelia's grave,
Harley nooses her hair around her own throat.

<64>

I, who cannot tolerate pen-clicking,
Fritos crunching, the nervous tapping of feet,
want this *frisson* of *frizuras* to vroom us,
screaming night hogs, through *Hamlet* —
stretching our scrunchies, our extensions, our do-rags.

Let's go ciliate silly, forsoothing over
every hirsutorufous, hirrient word —
as Hamlet cuts down Polonius, brushes off Gertrude.
Let's ride hairily with Harley in this Iron Butt Rally
for the old Ghost-Riding Ink-Slinging Hacker —

Will.

<65>

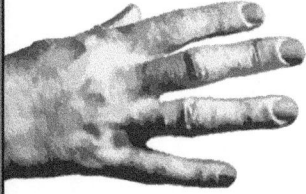

I V

IN
HOUSE

The End-All Diet

It will not be hard,
this diet —
no DVDs, no websites,
no *two-for-one*s at Jenny Dregs,
no Oldestra or Aspertime.
There will be no shame —

no temptation to binge and purge,
no eight glasses of water.
And starve — no more to starve.
It will be fast —
your thighs will never again strain
the zipper of your

jeans.
On its own, your belly will assume
that six-pack look — sucked in,
skin sculpting ribs.
Sit-ups will be strictly
forbidden.
The cellulite will unpucker

and dissolve.
Everyone will be waiting
to be as thin
as you in your
suit — size
zero, at last.

<69>

Hambugger, Inc:
The CEO Briefs Managers
On Employee-*hah* Relations

The prime directive is *keep 'em corralled*.
Stall 'em with barbs — give 'em something to beef about.
Beauty of it is — it'll make 'em come after you —
sure way to round up a herd.

Remember the stakes — they have no names.
Brand 'em! Makes head-counts a cinch
for ann'al retention review. And *PC*, my ass —
keep those no-account greenhorns in the dark —

you get whiter meat and more tender.
That's *Hay*ffirmative action if I ever heard.
APB 'bout broads and heifers — all teats and baloney —
their backtalk's bullshit — move it on out,

and in, and *howdeee*, while you're at it —
fertilize. . . Show 'em how the cow ate the cabbage.
When the union jerkies get all buck and horns —
stun and slaughter 'em in public. Grind 'em into patsies.

The rest are cowards — all of 'em —
they smell blood and huddle.
Tan their hides. Give 'em the boot.
Then browse around for some GMO-fed,

genetically man-i-pu-la-ted blood.
Let me reveal the secret of my success —
I pit bull against bull — keeps blood flowing.
The de-balled make the best cuts —

<70>

shell, strip, and blank. Once they're fixed
. . . well, I don't have to tell you.
Benefits and bonuses will just come
hoofing on in, ready for the barbeque —

grill 'em, lick 'em, fire 'em — marinate
their tongues. Feed them to each other.
Then dig in. No dilemma here. Believe you me —
ain't no such thang as Mad Cow.

<71>

Interview

Manicured fingers fist rings, thumb cells.
Four men Rolfe their elbows into my vita,
as if it were a placemat.
My interview suit fidgets

from my coccyx to my knotted neck.
They sit me in the preheated depressions
of another candidate's nervousness
and swirl my mind into a soup of names

(I could never remember), bubbles of eyes,
smiles of string beans.
My tongue swells into a ripe apple — too large
to form words, too slick to bite in time.

Then — one pinches my collar,
to decipher if I'm 100% or synthetic.
The business card they slip into my armpit
litmuses whether I'm poly- or un- saturated.

That something thin worming into my right ear —
coming out the left — is mental floss.
Two of them saw it back and forth
— slicing through the length of me —

and open me like a refrigerator
to see if the light turns on.
They inspect my drawers for uneaten spinach,
decades of unfinished glasses of milk.

<72>

They calibrate my tomatoes, toast my cold cuts and buns.
They unscrew my shelves with a dime and shake me
like a pinball machine — to see if they can score.
Meanwhile, I must keep cool, pre-shrunk,

so they can truss me with lines of policy,
baste me with a chorus of benefits.
Oiled up — the better to slide me through the mail slot
— I leave. They roll my vita into toothpicks and joints,

deliberate if 50K is too little, 70 too much —
like a commercial estimating prunes for regularity.
I wonder in my bed if I was the hole for their button,
the shell for their egg, the wallet for their wad of bills.

I rise, hungry, open my refrigerator,
empty but for something on the center rack —
— my face, my face —
I lean in. Stroke its lips.

<73>

Interoffice Memo   F Y I Need to Talk

Between us the cinderblock wall
Its sweat grit and empty cores
You puff *True Blues* and *Now*

To smoke a frame around your door
Where I wait to ask you
Again to open your window

You will belch the belch of one
Who has no need to state
My office my lungs my gut

Words to stun
My eyes will tug at your eyes
Don't gaze down the length of my hair

To my left breast
My hand a cameo at my throat
My elbow a shield

I'll say something about breathing
Tantric yoga you'll say
Best kind of breath   I won't

Understand   You'll say
All those naked yoga positions
I'll tell you love

Is a poem   You'll say
Emily Dickinson was an S&M
Lesbian black leather and studs

<74>

Under white piqué   I'll say
Love is an art
You'll say *Sex is a ribbed Trojan*

My ears like vacuums will draw
Forth your words to hang
Like swollen tongues from your lips

Your sentences will build around you
Like the cathedral of excrement
One tropical caterpillar

Sculpts around itself to say
To birds   *You don't want me   Please*
Don't eat me   I lift   now   my fist

Miss Liberty
Rock of desire   chisel of
Despair   strike the match

<75>

The Psychology of Rubbernecking

Helicopters *thump/thump/thump* like prehistoric dragonflies
over this junction of 24 and 78 — Something new. Something
up. Something *Something*. Fire trucks, patrol cars,

ambulances gyrate lights — whirling red, whirling blue,
whirling yellow — glittering, glinting, gleaming
on shattered glass — transforming smoke billows into multi-

colored cotton candy. They grieve. They keen. They run scales
from *oh* to *aaaeeeeeeeeee* — *oh weeeeeeee* — cosmic symphony
of *It's not me. It's not me. It's...* a car flipped over,

roof crushed in — no *way* anyone's alive in there —
the jaws of life no match for the single turn-signal blinking,
blinking — as if pulling back (I swear it looks like) tears...

and a truck jack-knifed — split clean apart — plumes of flames
grabbing at the choppers, like drowning hands. Behind them,
a millipede of sedan, SUV, convertible, truck, bus, motorcycle,

hatchback....Yet we, meant to move in the opposite direction,
are bumper-jammed, all gawk & cell — *I'm stuck, won't make it.*
Snap a shot. *Look. Look: Picked-off telephone pole, gushing*

<76>

*hydrant, car crumpled like a wad of Kleenex . . .*Instagrams
and Tweets of shrieking children, floating bodies, planes flying
into skyscrapers, American bombs bursting in mid-air —

necessary sacrifices, I suppose, to appease jealous gods,
that we, the saved again, watch, as if our eyes could
distance us from misfortunes that ransomed us

for our Bed, Bath, & Beyond lives — rescued us,
for the radical freedom of the open road —
put behind us an ever-receding God — lurking.

<77>

Meetings

When I've been *ad hoc*-ed and *in*
re-ed and briefed to death — our mugs
and cans stale around the table, and I'm
hovering like a thought balloon — I *nota bene*
the pencils: the Faber-Castell

seesawing on a fidget of fingers;
the Mickey Mouse dangling
from eraser ears, like a dowser's rod.
The pointillist that jackhammers
into a yellow pad — don't you know?

— it's the Morse of someone's pulse
pocked to the page. Count on the limbo
pole twirling under a nose:
that upper lip will never uncurl —
no matter.

And the new model from Leadworks, Inc.,
labeled, perhaps, *Miss Match Point*,
swatting words like a tennis racket
— all service and love —
will double-fault. Let it.

The boss is a cane tapping for curbs,
and the cooler buddy an automatic, clicking.
And the others — sharpened at both ends or
stubbed pointless — the Pinocchio nose,
the unicorn, the one gnawed to acne scars,

<78>

or aimed at a temple — all of us, *all*
are there for the Number 2, graphic
as ever. See it stuffing itself — *ram, ram,*
ram — into the mouth of a flexible straw:
that couldn't be me, getting rubbed out.

<79>

Night Work

Hardhat, overtime, road crew Jacks
float — tattered seraphim appearing and dis-
from wings of compressor steam;

thousand-watt halide floods; dust, dust,
dust from jack-hammerings at torn
asphalt, fissures, potholes, axle-

breaking ruts — depressions wrought by
straining heat, ice, time. These deities
of the reflective vest, Rough Rider gloves,

dark masks — near-death greeters tunneling
light — want to wrest us from our non-stop
go, and erect sand-filled channelizer drums —

those collapsible, orange and white,
Cat-in-the-Hat barrels — with pulsing arrows
funneling us — Hummers, Lexuses, Smart Cars,

Mini-Coopers, alike — into one unbreachable lane.
Faith was our smooth road — driving, entitled,
straight into futures — eternities without

cranes, forklifts, revolving concrete mixers
troubling our thrust. Doubt is this bumper jam —
our debt for being carried too long —

a clutter of trucks strobing lights as if
for a massive accident. Tired, idle — stalled —
I thrum the wheel, blinder my eyes from pockets

<80>

of sun pierced onto directional pales . . .
and take my one, last, momentary recourse —
before I, too, am corralled. I ignore the striped

attenuators, bravado the last free lane, pass the
willing Jeep, Ram, Yugo — dare the obedient Saab to
yield — then cut in hard to succumb to the drill.

<81>

The Darkest Evening of the Year

Snow is the road's ghost rising —
like my mother's frosts, her ice embrace,
the mists subliming in her wake —

raising the memory of prayer —
Blessèd be Airbags; Holy Anti-Locks; Praise be
Studded, Directional, Deep-Tread Goodyears.

Tonight, it's edgy weather and my worship
of the car thermometer that rides me —
not 32, stay at 33, please not freezing —

as if looking could warm a number
or what's falling on me —
Not hail. Not black ice. Grant me

gravity's grip . . . just 14 more minutes home.
Swirls nose the macadam like ectoplasmic hounds.
Strings of flakes arc toward my windshield,

beckon, like crooked fingers to follow —
as if my motion weren't creating
their *come* and *come.*

The wipers spank, pack, pound the snow
hard to the windshield's edge,
reducing the range of their sweep — *pig-in-a-*

poke, pig-in-a-poke. I turn off my inner blizzards —
the Lady GaGa CD slipped, like a communion host,
into the dash; the staticky Sirius weather terrorists;

<82>

(treads packed, rubber groaning with impacted snow)
to listen to my father's grumbling in my tires
— *Slow down. Keep moving. For traction.*

I'm afraid of the brake lengths between me
and 4x4s caging me from behind with their headlights;
afraid of slamming into rickety Fords

sneaking ahead on worn slippers —
white outs, spinning out, head-ons, stalls.
My daily fast-laning — to the *not-here,* the *not-there* —

is now a monkish squeeze to the right,
slow-crawling along the shoulder line,
my lights flashing *help me, help . . .*

<83>

Mating at Ruby Tuesday's — Friday Nights

Party of the First Part

Titles, torts, testimonies — his briefs
between us — Mick has asked me out for a bite —
a little something to chase the scramble
of our unisex week — this pub, a natural.

In any case, I'm a firefly with choices,
and Mick, talk-talking, could be a balloon fly
spinning for me, as lure, a fake mite from silk threads.
But here comes a CEO's son. *Look at me, not him,*

Mick seems to say, tugging his turtleneck over his
almost-wattle. This dewlap-flashing doesn't impress
me. He adjusts his horn-rimmed glasses, displaying
how much calcium he can metabolize over

his brain — *how smart, well-read, well-fed...*
I sing out to the CEO-apparent. Mick,
embarrassed, nibbles peanuts — false-
feeding like a spurned antelope. He sucks

in his gut, as if a hard, segmented beetle belly
would be lovely to me, while I'm smiling
up at the CEO-prince. Let Mick think this is
a case of female incitement — *fight*

for me so I can choose. On the walls
is a bowerbird scatter of trumpets;
a model ME109 Messerschmitt; crossed oars;
a blue Chevy tail fin, flashing its brake light.

<84>

Party of the Second Part

Despite the sisterhood of elephants,
girlfriend hyenas who outweigh the guys,
all the tail-feather-rattling peacocks
and neotropical frogs piggy-backing

their chunky females — *despite all that*,
Mick wants to fight for me. He shouts out to his rival —
be the bigger, stronger — divert this other guy,
say something I couldn't know: Jersey Devil stats,

NYSE options — something with numbers,
abbreviations. I know these, too, cut in, outscore.
If only Mick, like any self-respecting algae
or protozoa could manage to clone, dispense

with mates — or like wrasse swimming in
tropical waters, switch from being male
to female and back. If only he could stop pronking,
rebutting, swinging, strutting, he might notice

the CEO pup is gay; likes *him*, instead; is asking
from where *he* comes. And, droning the specials,
the tall waiter has ensnared me, *The Unkind*,
with his Stinger, in a glass unhooked, like a stalactite,

from the ceiling. He opens me
the menu of all the love that could never be —
the poached eggs, the curdled milks,
the fricasseed breasts, rumps, and fries.

<85>

I come and go among the voices
moaning from woofers and tweeters;
the Union Jack, draped, like harem silk,
from the ceiling; the glasses above, the men —

The Shrimp Fondue, Blondies, Crêpes.
How to *hang a name* on all the suits,
the bar, the claims — the hunger and the hung —
the *nothings gained, nothings lost.*

<86>

V

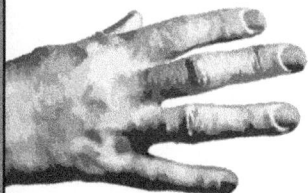

OUT OF THE HOUSE

Close

Silent, silent, silent
. . . Mother will be close at hand.
— Stevie Smith

A hand.
Your hand, Mother,

reaches up from my bed,
clutches at my thigh. I clasp...

your hand snaps off at the wrist.
I can't go. Can't stay. The bed

is heaped with your grasping:
piles of fingers at my head; racks

of wrists at my spine; elbows,
like rows of spearheads,

raying my feet. With your Kali
arms wrapped around my waist,

how to crawl back into myself?
How stop you from diving out

from between my legs, making of us
a two-headed spider? I push —

push at you — your body —
our body —

<89>

In Re: My Mother's Parole —

Your Honor, I am not my mother.
Her crimes? Count One: Kidnapping
my words to repeat to others

as if I were a babbling infant for her
to translate — she even repeats me
to my husband: *my husband.*

Count Two: Larcenies of his attention —
she fake-limps to take his arm,
goes gooey-dewy for him to pour her wine.

Only payback, she'd claim —
when I was sixteen she offered me
to her old boyfriends to enthrall them

back to her — dousing me with her Envy
Perfume, swathing me in her slips,
strangling my thighs with her garters —

making me her accessory, her Miss
"The Meaner," having me subpoenaed
for her men cheating on her.

That's Count Three: Child Exploitation.
And 4 — Whatever I do or am,
she Batters me to do better, other, else —

anything that'll make me into who she is:
not herself. Mostly, it's 5 — Negligence —
her sting to keep me gagged.

<90>

My mother's in lockdown in my body —
6 — clattering her tin cup
along the bars of my sleep,

shot-gunning my dreams.
She, 7 — Sues me with Frivolous Suits —
8 — Perjures herself, claiming Elder Abuse.

If the court permits, she'll work her 9 —
Embraceries on you officers, too.
I've had too much solitary with her.

Parole her, please, to some other district —
for my self-defense. I can't harbor
. . .

(Here, the advocate freezes. The mother cries out
through the daughter's mouth — *Habeas corpus!*
Under the influence! (Count to 10) *Miscarriage!*

<91>

Looking for You, My Half-Sister

1
Night beach, reek of burning in the air —
SUVs bobble in on softened tires
to ring, like Conestogas, bonfires of old

supermarket pallets, newsprint logs,
driftwood; and these mostly young couples,
newly rich, sitting at low green-clothed tables lit

by oil lamps, proffered champagne
by the caterer to whose wagon one
Hilfigered woman points me

when I ask what permit I
would need, from whom, to bring
my wood to burn on this sand.

2
A miniature ceramic Halloween house
appeared in the space where I parked.
Broken, yet all gables, bats,

and green-faced, warty witches
retrievable by tomorrow's glue —
it seemed so like a sign of something

(as if holding a place for me) —
as do the flames whipping
as if to hail ships lost at sea.

<92>

How wouldn't you be here, then,
on this night where people come
to float in summer white — you,

who refuses to know me;
you, who still has my nose, jaw,
my dark roots under L'Oréal?

3

Inhabit a body — my almost sister —
the young, the rich, the hot core
I might have been but for
what? That our father bought me
a white dress? That my kiss burned
your mother's cheek? I walk

the sand that's tamped stiff by receding tide —
pyre to pyre: the teepee of broken shelves,
the log cabin around a city in flames,

the steamer trunk flaring with slam-
dunked wine cups that score.
I would know you by your silhouette,

right shoulder hunched like your
mother's, the startled stay of your head
when you saw me.

<93>

4

Dangled from a bamboo rod shoved
through the arms of a lifeguard stand,
is a blond Raggedy Ann piñata

in blue-checked pinafore. A crowd
rings around it, spins a blindfolded
woman in circles, who caroms

between anonymous arms to push her
toward the doll. *To your left,* voices cry out,
straight... She staggers — *another*

step — in the dip of sand, the woman who
cannot see, with a baseball bat in her hands.
Go — get her, they yell as she flails,

striking the air so, sometimes, she
smacks her own legs —
spins, stumbles. *White Trash,* they chant

Die, White Trash. A blow. The doll
yields — swings safe. The woman reaches
her hand as if to say *Stay. It's all right.*

It's to steady her mark. She swings
hard, high, catches the left cheek —
silver-foiled kisses rush out;

<94>

and Life Savers, individually wrapped,
which no one will have. Forward, the others
press, to have the Ace wound over their eyes:

a man, who — although the doll is spent —
will bat and bat and bat until her crêpe face
tears, flies in shreds to bank in the fire's drafts.

5
A blue paper eye floats up, then down —
its black half moon iris caressing
a white circle. I slip it into my jeans

for a handkerchief. Then pluck it out,
like a magician, to conjure you looking
at me, frozen by the fire.

Taking Photographs

My mother's Canon Sure Shot lens opens
into a cosmic hole sucking in my front door.
Already, she's taken the pin oak from the lawn.

She lowers her camera to size up her next frame,
dives back behind that single eye
in time for me to jump away.

Pop — she takes my newel post,
newly stripped of forty years of paint,
butcher-waxed to a lustrous sheen;

and *snap* — there go my UGGs,
lined up so neatly for her coming.
Zoom, zoom — to the *Ladies' Room* —

she squeezes off my eggshell Belgian sink,
then to my bedroom to shed the down parka
I hand-me-upped to her;

and to gulp my bed, my stuffed Bugs Bunny,
my Buddha-bellied ape.
My closet, where hung my red Marilyn dress

is Cyclops *schlurp.*
My study where hung my crystal heart is
flash — the void.

<96>

She mugs my husband's desk, his chair,
The Herald that was hiding him —
him. She photographs the *dahl* I stewed for her,

the potpourri wafting pine and myrrh,
and *oops* — she shoots herself
and the camera in the mirror.

There she floats, a single eye —
hungry, unblinking,
exposed.

<97>

My Mother's Head

1

is bowed, not for some holy robe, nor long nod
of *yes*, nor sleep, nor shame.

Age, let's call it, as of this headless woman
(or so she seems, her neck's so bent),
in the *King's Supermarket* parking lot.

She's Alice's Mock Turtle reared on hind legs,
head sucked into her shell, front flippers propped
on the empty chrome basket.
She's wheeling past beached SUVs —
heading for the automatic doors —
a body functional though there's
a neat line of shoulder where . . .

2

I'm stopped at a red light
when I see this woman who might be
my mother if I don't intervene.
Of course, she *must* have a head —
the woman behind the cart — and a mouth
and eyes — you need them to shop —
ears would help, a nose.

<98>

3

A dream: *The Anne Boleyn HQ for the Decephalized.*
Slogans fly on flag poles: *Lost Our Heads, Heads
Off.* Everywhere, heads roll where lost heads go —
The Venus de Milo Holding Tank —
waiting to be transplanted onto bodies:

a derrick lowers a Barbie face
onto the broad shelf of a sumo
ventriloquizing *I want to wrestle a virtual Ken*;

a tattooed lady shoulders a lama's depilated scalp
chanting *Prick an ink Medusa into my OMM*;

a head-advantaged nurse leads my mother's body
down a corridor, like a bride.

4

I'm alone, idling at this light.
My mother's making frog-eyes
over the surface of some Budapest Turkish bath.
From inside my thalamus my husband whispers:
She won't wear bifocals —
that's why she has to bow her head.
Vain — eighty two, but vain.
True, she squeezes her glasses down so hard
they wrinkle her nose like an elephant's knee.
Old. Don't give in — I whisper in my head.
She raises

<99>

5

hers — her turn to pick a card at my kitchen table.
We're playing Robber Rummy, stealing from melds
fanned between us, remaking our own runs
of mixed suits, and unbroken flushes.
Yes, *flushes*, I know.
But it's not as though she *can't* hold her head up
(please not that). No bone in her neck effervesced,
as mine might from guzzling decades of Royal Crown.
Old, I taunt her, *lift up your head.*
She furls it like a time-lapsed fern in reverse.
She draws a card, looks up at me
from under penciled eyebrows;

6

I'm not ready for my cheek pressed
to my steering wheel, the better to see
the supermarket woman.
Give me some sign of face;
a wisp of permed blue cottonball hair;
a glint of cabochon clipped to an ear.
She's pressing ahead.

7

My own head is bent, at the kitchen table,
and craned to espy my mother's eyes.
Let my eyes lift yours.
Old, I say, pleading.
Right, she says, from her question-mark body,
You're right.
Here it comes, all I've needed for her to say:

<100>

8

her head is bent in *grief*. Yes, she grieves —
she is strong enough to grieve —
for the gymnast she couldn't (*didn't* —
more power) let herself be,
double-somersault-twisting off a four-inch beam,
back arched, arms Veed in Victory,
head back. Or, let's face it,
that she's ashamed for _____
[here insert how she didn't mother me].
In any case, let her wilt her head
for something that means *something* —
that gives me a flicker — any sign of will
or its breaking,

9

and not the *King's* automatic doors
opening for a woman who lets herself be
swallowed by overhead neons
before I can know her and my light
turns.

<101>

The Pregnant Husband

*Pregnancy didn't prevent him
from being a model husband.*
                    — The Huffington Press

Breasts flattened to trans *she* to *he*,
Thomas Beatie poses — a bearded Madonna,
right hand at his nape, shock of manly armpit hair;
left hand on his 22-week belly.

My mother, too, was once a woman
like Elizabeth Taylor, my father said,
pointing to a photograph of her hiding
her pregnant belly with a manila folder.

Now, my mother swells a Bud gut,
beats my stepfather at Robber Rummy.
To lose her breasts, she lies about mammograms.
The surgeon delivers *gefilte*-sized yellow lumps.

My stepfather's stomach *couvades* with ulcers.
He wears a high apron for my mother,
bakes Black Forest tortes, buys beaded gowns
to dangle tags in the closet.

He and I sing *Phantom of the Opera*
and anything Cher, antique for 70s platform shoes,
argue over what color to dye his hair.
Love, be who you are — no matter.

<102>

Sitting with Grandmother on a Park Bench

She's wearing her instant facelift —
long rubber-bands taped at her temples;
tied, like apron strings, behind her head.
Her strawberry-blond Zsa Zsa wig
clutches her scalp like a shriveled starfish.

A homeless man — bald,
but for his thin gray ponytail —
sits on the ground, leans on a willow,
plucks at a broken zither.

She steadies a gutted coconut half on her knees,
sprinkles in one pink plastic rosary bead,
toothpicks gnawed the required nine times,
half-moon nail parings she douses with honey.

She is humming "Hungarian Rhapsody"
following and not following
the homeless man's notes.
He's Liszt, she says, *come to marry me.*

Nothing I can do for her —
whose first husband died of a stroke;
whose second, soldier husband,
was run down by a truck —

but believe with her that she is young again,
sitting by the Danube, and that I am her sister.
Look, I whisper to her, *that man with long fingers —
he's come back for you, your Franz.*

<103>

Not brushing my teeth

is all I have left, sometimes, of freedom and lust —
this sweet, sweet potato-ing on the couch —
this *Get up! Get up!* yielding to *Nahhh.*

Why bother? Tuna, sesame, celery
(the occasional gnat), and germs
shuttling on rafts of words
anchor so like popcorn shells

in my bridgework and gaps,
I might need razor wire for floss,
and calculus to figure how to winch
these feet onto the floor...

And the remote has fallen between the cushions,
Dark Shadows is rerunning on the tube —
ocean waves cresting and dashing
against the rotten-teeth rocks of the shore.

Barnabas Collins is baring his bloody fangs.
Clean teeth would glow to him —
a come-on of my vampire virginity.
No, it's too scary to move.

Really, how much could my gums recede
from one day of unabluted mastication,
one night of voyeuring and not doing
the commercials' bidding —

not squeezing the Crest; not slipping the rubber
Butler — *wiggle wiggle* — into my cracks;
not back-and-forthing the floss
through my amalgamated crevices?

<104>

And plaque? Let it do what plaque does —
build. This is my forbidden, at last:
sugars tingling through pulp-embedded nerves,
the illicit lingering with the undigested,

tongue sucked to my palate in redolent marination.
So what! to the tartar I might catch
for my night on the cusp of taboo,
for not brushing off inevitable decay.

<105>

Waldo, Where is My Mother?

Like looking for you, whom I, no matter, spot
in The Nasty Nasties Castle
massed with mummies, zombies, ghouls;
in the toque-jammed Cake Factory;
in the Wild, Wild West with gallons of hats,
saloon doors, and Colts,

I am looking for my mother in what isn't me
— men, men, men — maybe in The Black Forest
of antlers, bucks, rummage of pants, beards.
Has she slipped on my father's vest,
my second stepfather's belt?
Has she grown whiskers?

Maybe she's in The Clown Carnival —
her posey-pursed faced peeking out
from Pavarotti's cut-out. But if
my mother were my mother
she'd be a cut-up, instead.
Waldo, are *you* my mother,

my Emissary of Elusion in Male Drag?
In the lie-down prisoner-striped stovepipe
slipped over her body. Oh, Waldo, I know
it can't be you, for *You* live for me to find you.
I always know I will. And know when I have.

<106>

VI

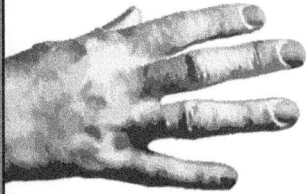

THE HOUSE OF WORDS

Druid Diary

— After artist Julie Harris's "Druid Diary"

The book never forgets to be
the tree — to sheathe itself in stiff bark,
to fill with rings of separation.

The book gathers back its twigs —
bookmarked, as it is, by protruding pencils, toilet paper,
torn envelopes — its pages proverbially dog-earred.

The book admits it is pulp — fibers
clotting to fibers, speckled with foxing,
blooming in drops of tea, milk, blood.

The book wraps itself in eyes and hands and eyes —
ready to open anywhere, to welcome lead
and ink, to yield to leafing.

The book yearns to soft us in its baleen;
to comb us, like waterfalls. The book is lung
rippling the air, fannnig out in wings.

The book knows what it means to wait,
to press against other books, to stand —
to have its spine broken, to be silent.

<109>

The House of Words

is a woman without a home —
Eve shaking the tree, back
arched, leaves floating.

Isis breathes moon and stars
into our ears. Mary pens
life from decay.

We enter, as we must,
to climb into Emily's dome,
to slip into the river of words

Virginia built for a roof.
This house is a place
of wandering:

Edith sailing Lily from
less to less; Jane burning
what was — for what can be.

The house of words is the welcome
that empties itself, to
refill; the coming that goes

to come. Line by line
we descend to find
our homelessness —

tear down the gables of grief,
rend the casements of loss,
rebuild ourselves

<110>

on the broken ground of hope,
and the mortar of memory.

Ceiling, scribing, yoke and span;
sash, keeper, stairs and nails —
we strut, lumber, barge, rail.

<111>

Eaten by Stars: An Elegy for Allen

> *O roar of the universe, how am I chosen?*
> *. . . I am ready to die.* — Allen Ginsberg, "The Lion for Real"

Allen, our Earth eclipses the sun to cast —
on this, your last night, an Oreo moon.
Like too much love, the bright sphere creams
around the edge of the chocolate disc.

Overlook on Route 80, before Exit 19,
above the mountains — Hale-Bopp —
The Great Comet — millennial smudge coursing
from Leo toward Orion and his sword of stars.

39 people of Heaven's Gate Higher Source Group
(one for each whipping stroke of Christ),
eat phenobarbital-laced applesauce,
pull plastic bags over their faces

to hitch a ride on a UFO forged
into a picture of your Halley's —
portentous as the Star in the East
or Twain's comet-framed life.

At Disney World, spigots, like landmines,
wait among spotlights recessed into the ground.
A black-haired, four-year-old boy walks
among them, deliciously not wanting

and still wanting for the *it* to happen —
the triggered geysers, the shocks
of water shooting up. All six spigots gush
at last, to his one-enough step.

<112>

Hands to his face, impossibly wet, he *is*
this eruption coming up between his legs —
he *is* this illuminated spring standing there;
the white column of water, his spine;

streams falling away like arms; watery head
bobbling on top. He screams, he howls
from the not having to not howl.
At my rest stop, with too many cars speeding

behind, and enough stars, a Mack Truck *OM*s
like a shofar, like a Tibetan long horn elbowing
the ground. I swear, Bubba, all of us —
Orion beckoning to Leo, the Oreo moon halo-ing

a full circle smile, the flying suicides,
and your Be-Bopp Comet —
like the Disney geysers, like the little boy,
like the hills themselves that have known

only waiting 'til now — all of us echoèd,
echoèd, Allen, as you rose,
as the heavens licked you up,
as you rushed into the stars.

<113>

An Erotics of Poetry Intensives

Starve them a little to make them keen.
— Robert Dudley, in Bette Davis's
The Private Lives of Elizabeth and Essex

Chattery Harvard sylph, heel tucked under her butt,
next to gray Bacchus, who's tasting aloud her poem titled
"Untitle" — fourth time, now, the arrow tip of his tongue
lingers on the brink of the missing *d*.

"So unexpect...!" he quips, grins to make her grin,
reads on, pupils spreading like ink re her enjambment on
the — he calls it "the suicidal crest of your roller-coaster
lines," and then, glancing at her bent knee

under her papers, adds "Your vowel movements...
love how you come up with...the plaintive airs."
He clicks his ballpoint out, in, out. "Let me have it —
your cell," he says, "Can we friend?"

Next to her, the Nam vet nods, the ponytailed
60-something DJ triple *uh-hum*s. "Of course,"
Bacchus says, "I'm taking everyone down."
And it's not the easy statutory lay he wants,

but the easing down of the sylph's tongue,
the slight opening, now, of her silenced lips;
and the woman next to her, who could be her
mother. With each rapture about Harvard's

"ecstatic collages," the skin of this crone-
in-training beads up along the edges of her L'Oreal.
She's cupping her jowls with her left hand,
scooping at her bra strap with her right.

<114>

Bacchus strokes the co-ed's page to make
the crone's crayoned eyebrows droop,
to make the "please take **me**" bloom in her eyes.
Six times, he makes her raise her hand for her

turn, then double-speeds through her only copy,
tells her she's taking no risks, is "not opening up."
And he waits for it — her neck flushing up into her cheeks,
the puckering of her chin, and then the practiced

stretching of it down. The thought of her voice
blubbering tonight through the bathroom door
is like a goatskin of Dry Sack to him.
He surveys the sylph's thinning breath,

the vet jabbing his pencil into his spiral-bound's coil,
the DJ he'll spin next, and her, waiting, again.
He hesitates — oh that pause — then gives it to her:
"I only want to take you — to the next level."

<115>

Dancing with The Camera
At The Dodge Poetry Festival

Practice making the unwanted wanted.
— Jane Hirshfield

The camera dangles from the end of its long boom —
a creature infinitely wanting, infinitely curious;
a handkerchief brushing the poet's breath
into the velvet breath of the thousands before her.
Of course, the listeners' faces the camera questions,
when it veers toward them, tighten
into *intelligent eyes, sensitive mouths,*
and *will-it-capture-me-for-a-Bill-Moyers-Special?* ignorings.
It backs up, now, as if from royalty,
turns to jockey the poet's resolve to *not-care* —
all that *mustn't look* for, *look* into *what looks at me.*

Poems of will, poems of imagination —
the devastation of facing God's hunger and Death's —
the poet looks, instead, onto her page,
and up into the tiered sequins of eyes,
feels the waiting-room of lights scudding behind her ...
and the camera glides on its counter-balanced bridge,
anchored by weights of anonymity, spanning
the River Memory, hovering to clear the masts
of all that longing for, and terrors of not being known.
Phallic in thrust, yonic in taking, the camera knows

how to love a poet, to trace the back of an ear, to settle
almost on a shoulder like a phantom violin
bowing to what's behind. It narrows its lens
to peer onto the poet's bright page, and widens
to gaze into the semi-dark of the audience waiting,
waiting for the poet to word, word, word of things not here.

<116>

Like God, the camera surveys all in its entitlement,
its glory in not needing to be seen.
It dives now to wag at the poet's feet, puppying her
to forget the page, reach down to touch . . .

She mustn't let on, of course, that she wants to be loved —
to be the poet is to *be* the camera — free of the ascendant
Adam *I, me, mine* that troubles the hidden —
what? Even to name it is . . . Poetry must play hard-to-get.
But what's been lost? What does it take to *not* recognize
this twenty-foot bionic giraffe licking at the poet's lightz
Cropping at the motes she swirls? This time, let her cover
her page. Let her turn to look into the void of notoriety.
The camera might dodge her eyes, shake itself, retract —
roll its Cyclops eye to stare up at the tent's ribs.

But the poet takes the camera by its handles, faces it
like a lover. She leads — when she turns, it turns.
When she ducks — it ducks. Dip for dip — step for sidestep —
its meters hers. Waltz, funk, salsa — dizzy embracing
the forbidden. And the listeners sway to their *pas de deux*,
rise, clatter their chairs in applause, fill the aisles.
The poet mounts the boom, bronchos it like a cow-witch.
She and the camera soar. They body surf the hands
reaching for them. The shutter blinks/blinks in gratitude.

In time, the poet will seem to alight, again, behind the podium.
Wanting the one who wants to be unwanted,
she will make a lens of her mouth
and let the audience be taken — with her.

<117>

A Poet's Luck

— To artist Robin Landa,

"Poets are lucky," you say,
"They can write anywhere.
No need for brush or canvas or space."

But Robin, do your brushes, like my words, fray from
conducting dusty meetings, until their edges
untrue, jam too mote-gritty for paint?

Do your sables wax hard from licking, licking,
at lingo-locked ears? Ram, gavel their flame tips
in political potpourris until, splat asterisks,

they limn shadows, at best? And what if
your canvas — like my freedom —
were pot-holed by interoffice *ASAPs*?

What if your frames twisted trapezoidal negotiating
Delta and WalMart checkouts — your anticipation
pothered with distempers of robocalls,

Blue Cross, and phone menus? No sure
turpentine unbristles my words to exult
in an atelier's soft light. My frames must

be remitered from broken parts of potluck
splinters. May you never have to watch your cochineals
coagulate with the jet critics pot shot

into their bright lakes. When last did your jades
have first to realchemize
by painting how hard it is to paint?

<118>

Breaking Ball

Some writers like to use the word stanza *for* inning,
but I don't. Baseball is a sport, not poetry.
— David H. Martinez, *The Book of Baseball Literacy*

But David, poetry is a sport, not baseball —
and it's for the boys. Who's always up
but the Collinses and Dickeys?
When it's Olds, it's that she has a bat,

so to speak, in every poem.
No, the Babe in the bullpen is the ballgirl.
Stevie, Anne, Sylvia had to strike
themselves out for a scoring position

in the major leagues of all-time.
Emily had to make an appeal play
of her shut out. Come on, guys,
of course poetry is a sport. Why else

do I wind up winding up pompons in the stands?
I get The Lip for my line drives.
My hot doggerels are checked in a hawking tray.
At best, like Pam, I'm an ump in the Triple As,

out of the box, always behind the plate. Oh
change-up Sadaharu Oh for *Oh Susanna*
when poetry is not just a sport but is
baseball — the growing of green turf

around our altar of dust —
the hush, The Big Hurt,
the crack, the song —
the ball we watch like the Sun —

<119>

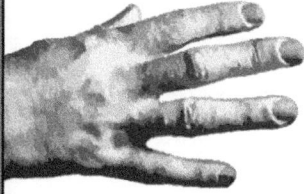

VII

DOLL HOUSE

Sundown in the Town Called "Mother"

after *High Noon*

Must I be cast as the outlaw Frank Miller,
sentenced for a crime I can't remember?
Mother, did I kill the young woman you were?
Did I create the cancer that broke your chest
into one saloon door unhinged, one squealing?
Did I shatter the long mirror behind the bar
so I can't see myself, so I can't watch
for who's coming from behind?

I am not the judge, packing up my books,
to escape the thug hurting for revenge.
And, the townspeople have fled.
Tumbleweed haunts the abandoned streets.

If only I could be Marshal Will — taking off my spurs,
grinding my tin star into the dust — I could sit
at the judge's desk, write your last testament.
But I must be Frank — the camera closing in
on the empty chair where I was given life.

<123>

best-alzheimers-products.com/serenity-babies

I am your Therapy Doll, Mother.
I am sculpted of heirloom quality materials.
You can yank my stranded, micro-rooted hair.
I am weighted with glass beads
for better hurling at the television.

I will lie wherever you want.
I will say *Mama, Mama,* in an adoring voice.
I don't require pampering. I never bawl.
You can hide me under the sink.
I stay and stay still.

I will never talk back, at, or over you.
I will never sass you to eat or to walk or to rest.
We won't need that daughter-woman by the door.
She is too big; she doesn't thrive on batteries;
she cannot be charged.

<124>

Chimera

The Q-Tip I make my mother swish inside her cheeks.
The orange-and-white striped specimen Ziplock.

Biohazard the bag says, in a red circle;
and *Remember* with an icon of crossed fingers.

The Genetic Open Discovery Email says
it's 99.9998% reliable that she's your mother.

Human chimerism, I had hoped — genes skipping
a generation — be related to my grandmother — not her —

my *chimera* — momster — half lion head,
half dragon butt.

The service called *A Place for Mom* phones:
How's your Mom?

Your Mom, my therapist says, voice cuddly,
after months of my begging, *Don't call her Mom.*

One mothering *mother* from his mouth —
he's back to *Mom.*

But there's no *mmmm* here — no *Ommm*
in my *moth*, my *other*, my *her.*

<125>

Battleground Mother

Achieve Rehabilitation Center
Liberty, New York

Parkinson's: hands shaking ghost hands,
thumbs and forefingers pill-rolling,
neck bent horizontal,
right eye lidded, urine bag.

You hallucinate infant me on the toilet,
and my stepfather's head floating in a drawer.
He swallows fourteen Tylenols, attempting
to escape your going back home.

But then he asks everyone,
Why can't old people die
when they want to?
and attempts to kidnap you.

I'm afraid he'll kill you both.
Twice daily, I erase his voice mail barrage.
I wrested medical proxy from him;
I want you to live.

I cry on the phone to your brother.
He's pissed he's not in your will,
so he yells, then stonewalls me.
His children unfriend me on Facebook.

<126>

I drive four hours to you in early morning dark
to dodge my stepfather's ambush.
And, oh, the lines drawn for these spoils —
you among my desiccated spider mums;

the aides making their sneaker rounds
with shots and expired magazines;
these wet sheets; the words we don't say:
You're mine. Mine.

<127>

the ventriloquist

when the body dies
where is the presence then
— Alfred Corn

grandma I am trying
to press your body
into your coffin   but your
arms   legs   head keep
spilling like a dummy's
out

I squat on your lid like a paperweight
wedge in your arms with my hands
your bunioned feet with mine
tuck in your dyed hair
with my teeth   mound dirt
on

just when you seem
all cozy in the ground
an earlobe
or nipple comes
cropping like a dandelion
up

so I mulch your grave
with photographs
condolence cards   obits
but you are belting out dirty songs
that will not go
away

<128>

shall we exhume you
buy you a new plot
for a place distant
from the neighboring dead
so they can lie back
down

beyond mortified   I move
to a mountain   and slowly
I turn to find you conducting
the birds and frogs
in your poltergeist sing
along

belly breathing in the trees
tweeting and croaking with
you   grandma jane in the box
playing this to the back row
so listen   did you hear the one
about

<129>

The *Dybbuk*

Dybbuk — from the Hebrew for "adhere" or "cling" —
is the evil spirit of a dead person who is not laid to rest,
enters into a living person, cleaves to her soul,
causes mental illness, talks through her mouth.
                    — Paraphrased from Jewish Virtual Library

1
You die alone, Mother. That moment,
a bat appears in Mort's room — wakes me
shrieking from an unnatural nap, swoops
at me through the hallway, the dining,
the living room — I say it is you
and it's gone.

The gilt clock your husband gave us stops
on the moment of your death. My framed
website photo smashes to the floor.
A seven-foot driftwood trunk topples,
missing me by four inches. Snow, wind,
midnight power-outs — clocks flashing wrong,
different times.

The cemetery is too frozen
to receive you, who hoarded towers
of sour cream cups, Hungarian
newspapers, 436 knitted caps —
are hoarding, still — your sealed
coffin in the funeral home cooler,
for three months.

<130>

2

Night of your funeral mass, Mort can't walk —
ER, surgery — ureter cut
by mistake — his belly swollen to a ten-month
gravid bowling ball.

My Al Anon sponsor divorces me —
by text. One best friend is diagnosed
with breast tumors; another falls twice
in the night, breaking her neck and foot.

My black cat dies, the hot water stops, mice
overrun our silverware drawers,
the dryer duct burns.

3

The film *The Unborn*, on Lifetime
Channel, a twin *dybbuk* kills lovely
Casey's grandmother, then her best friend,
then her lover — to weaken Casey enough
to enter her body — be reborn.

4

Images of *dybbuks*: hand thrusting
out of a mouth, a dog's head upside
down, double heads, man-of-war suckling
on a man's nipples, a skeleton lying
on a girl.

<131>

5

Your husband insists — April 30 for your burial,
not knowing it's Walpurgis Night,
the Halloween of Spring; and my father's
and stepmother's 46th anniversary.
I gas up. The receipt reads 6.66 gallons:
666 — Revelations: 13,
mark of the beast, Nero's numerals,
he who sent his mother out in a
faulty ship to drown, and played the lyre
while Rome burned.

So I veer toward the Massachusetts
Poetry Festival. 11:00 AM,
as they lower your coffin
into a small New York village grave,
I, at the pulpit of the Salem church called
The Bridge, sing "Think of Me"
from *The Phantom of the Opera.*

6

In a dream, I say that I welcome
the ancestors. A white sun descends
to fill my eyes and face. I wake up
hearing your voice in my mouth — the last
words no one heard, as you died, alone —
Help me! Please!

<132>

< Scissors

Caesar was called "Caesar," because scissored
(from the Latin *cisoria)* from his mother's belly.

Still, I carry blue-handled scissors everywhere,
but, in an emptied Kleenex tis-sue box,
are 41 pairs of scissors my mother hoarded in her ga-
rage. Ones pi-voted on sin-gle screws include
4 stain-less steel pairs with black ears, pain-
t worn from hand sweat; 2 pin-king shears with s-
hark tooth blades; 6 blunt no-sed quack-quacks,
for no-body's children; needle-pointed cuticle scis-sors;
one p-air stork scissors, blades so swung open the dull
edges meet; and two car-pet scis-sors, like pelicans
on the wing. The most elegant is the Italian *Premana*
pair, spring loaded, one thumb-sized hole, like a mouth,
for stea-dying. Plus there're the 10 pairs Mort
culled as us-eful, that he just can't seem to find now.
All these scis-sors, shut into them-selves, pivot
screws like goat eyes above o-pen jaws clack- snipp-
shear- ripp- ing in applause; not cutting up, down,
through a way. Whe-never I spoke with my moth-
er th-rough the phone's pin holes, and she did, could,
would not hear me, didn't want to k-now ___,
I yelled to Mort to hide our scis-sors —
I needed so-me-thing to turn on my-self —
like these ovarian handles with vaginal blades
that my mother left me in her tissue box **>**

<133>

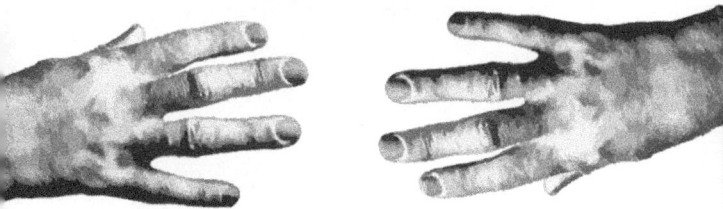

HAUNTED
HOUSE

EPILOGUE

The Thing: *My Crazy Family*

> *Poisonous ideals ...*
> — Robert Haas and Brenda Hillman

Who needs a Pillsbury-Dough-Boy daddy
nice-nice-ing sunshine up your hot cross buns?
Or a *doo doo doodoo* Martha Stewart mom making you
Snap! Snap! to her will, double-sticking it to you
about her goody-goody good things? Nah,
the Addams Family taught me *my crazy family* had it right:

we live in dungeon dreams of Brady-Bunch belonging.
Snap! Snap! off the reeky rose heads of a Hallmark Card life —
that *Father Knows Best doodoo* others *televise* they have.
Caress, instead, as Morticia does, the thorns —
those lush dependable claws of lust, sloth, greed, envy,
hate, rage, and grief that last, unlike petals, and last. *Snap!*

Snap! out of your float down the River Denial and be free.
Confess! Surreal and funereal is realer than real.
Your *doo doo doodoo* grandmama *is Snap! Snap!*-ing daggers
at her son, her daughter-in-law, and her grandchildren.
Your suave Daddy would rather stay home sucking on his
doo doo doodoo Cubanitos rolled in stocks.

Your uncle is a festering conduit of charges —
a remake of Betty's *boop-oop-a-doop* Grampy flashing
light bulbs. Are you saying *My crazy family is going to make me
Snap! Snap!*? Then, you are, as I am in *my crazy family*:
the official Thing T. Thing, this give-us-a hand jane-
or jack-in-the-box, dismemberment — this member meant

<137>

for delivering *doo doo doodoo* ego rubs, for dusting secrets
off the table. Come dirty! Fess up! It's a *Snap! Snap!*
to make-wrong, to back-scratch only to be back-scratched
(preferably with a two-handed back-scratcher), to bitch and snarl
my crazy family. Harder to be, as I am — as thing as Thing.
But I have no skittering Cousin (*dee dee dee*) Itt; no Lurch

intoning *You rang? You rang?* and being that someone
to turn pages for, to play for me, pay for me.
To secure your place in the family all you need to *doo
doo doodoo* is make a face irrelevant, a voice...
Unnamed and unnameable, be for them the one hand
doodoo-ing them on. But keep the other to yourself —

out of the boxed-in, dangling a dervish spin-
spinning yourself into the beloved — the beloved.
And then conduct yourself, as I do, one hand firmly
on the bible of *my crazy family*, the other a floating cursor
on my PC, an illusionist detached, prestidigitating
my crazy family to appear and then, *doo doo doodoo* —
Snap!

<138>

ABOUT THE AUTHOR

Susanna Rich is a bilingual Hungarian-American, Fulbright Fellow in Creative Writing, and Collegium Budapest Fellow — with roots in Transylvania and family ties to the Blood Countess, Elizabeth Báthory. She is a Distinguished Professor of English Studies at Kean University (NJ), with a dynamic teaching blog, becauseicanteach.blogspot.com. Susanna is also an Emmy Award nominee, and the founding producer and principal performer at Wild Nights Productions, LLC. Her repertoire includes the musical *Shakespeare's *itches: The Women v. Will,* and *ashes, ashes: A Poet Responds to the Shoah.* She is author of three earlier poetry collections, *Television Daddy* and *The Drive Home* (Finishing Line Press), both of which are also Wild Nights performances; and *Surfing for Jesus* (Blast Press). Visit Susanna at www.wildnightsproductions.com.

<139>

ACKNOWLEDGMENTS

I am grateful to the editors of the following publications for first printing these poems, often in earlier versions.

Birmingham Poetry Review: "We're Fringed"
Crucible: "Not Brushing My Teeth"
Darkling: "From a Mother in the Garden of Grief"
Dream: "Sundown in the Town Called 'Mother'"
English Journal: "Multiple Seed: To Students Writing in Response to Williams's *Paterson*"
Feminist Studies: "Grandmother Sausages"
Folly Magazine: "The Thing"
Journal of New Jersey Poets: "Dancing with the Camera at the Dodge Poetry Festival."
New Millennium Writings: "The Trees Are Falling Because They Must"
Pennsylvania English: "Sitting with Grandmother on a Park Bench" (as "Fourth Street")
Phoebe (Fairfax): "possession." and "ventriloquist"
Phoebe (Oneonta): "My Mother's Kitchen is her Pontiac"
The Poetry Review: "Adopt-a-Corpse"
Presence: "Combing Through *Hamlet*"
Sanskrit: "The End-All Diet"
Sensations Magazine: "The Abandoned House," "Anchor," "The Hidden Mother," "Looking for You, My Half-Sister," "Night Work," "Piñata," "The Pregnant Husband," and "Puddling"
Skidrow Penthouse: "My Mother's Head"
South Coast Poetry Journal: "The Buck" and "Taking Photographs"
Southern California Review: "Meetings"
Spitball: "Breaking Ball"
Studio One: "A Baby Sister"
The Teacher's Voice: "Hambugger, Inc."

<141>

This Broken Shore: "The *Dybbuk*," "An Erotics of Poetry Intensives," and
    "The Psychology of Rubbernecking"
Urthona (UK): "Requiem for a Terrorist's Hands"
The Vocabula Review: "A Poet's Luck"
Willow Review: "Daddy, First Communion Sunday, *Lassie*," "Playgirl"

"Baby Sister" also appears in *Soundings* and *Willow Review.*
"Beware the House with No Corners" appears in *Poets of the Palisades.*
    Eds. Paul Nash and Denise LeNeve. Pittsburgh: The Poet's Press,
    2016.
"The Buck" also appears in *Writers on the Water's Edge.* Ocean Grove:
    Tri-Muse, 2003; in *Poem, Revised.* Ed. Robert Fiske. Oak Park:
    Marion Street P; in *Darkling,* and in *Surfing for Jesus.* Susanna
    Rich. Red Bank: Blast Press, 2017.
"Close" appears in *Off Line: An Anthology of New Jersey Poets.* Ed.
    Judith Christian, 2011.
"Daddy, First Communion Sunday, *Lassie*" also appears in *Television
    Daddy.* Susanna Rich. Georgetown: Finishing Line Press, 2009; and
    Surfing for Jesus. Susanna Rich. Red Bank: Blast Press, 2017.
"Dancing with the Camera at the Dodge Poetry Festival" also appears in
    Dance Anthology. Ed. Johnny M. Tucker.
"Fly in Our Classroom" appears in *Voices from Here 2.* Sparta:
    Paulinskill Poetry Project. (2017): 159.
"Grandmother Sausages" also appears in *Writers on the Water's Edge.*
    Ocean Grove: Tri-Muse, 2003; and *Hymns to the Outrageous.*
    Johnstown: Pudding House Press; and *Television Daddy*, by
    Susanna Rich. Georgetown: Finishing Line Press, 2009.
"The House of Words" appears in *Meta-Land: Poets of the Palisades II.*
    Pittsburgh: The Poet's Press, 2016. 185-6.
"Interoffice Memo: F Y I Need to Talk" appears in *Mentor & Muse.* Ed.
    Blas Falconer et al. Carbondale: Southern Illinois UP, 2010.
"Interview" appears in *If I Had a Hammer.* Ed. Sandra Martz.
    Watsonville: Papier Mâché P, 1990; and in *Administration &
    Management.*
"My Mother's Kitchen is Her Pontiac" also appears in *The Drive Home*, by
    Susanna Rich. Georgetown: Finishing Line Press, 2008.
"Not Brushing My Teeth" also appears in *The Dos Passos Review*; and
    Television Daddy, by Susanna Rich. Georgetown: Finishing Line
    Press, 2009.
"Playgirl" also appears in *Television Daddy.* Susanna Rich. Georgetown:
    Finishing Line Press, 2009.
"Requiem for a Terrorist's Hands" also appears in *The Drive Home*, by
    Susanna Rich. Georgetown: Finishing Line Press, 2008.

<142>

"Sitting with Grandmother on a Park Bench" also appears as "Fourth Street" in *U.S. 1* Worksheets.

"The Thing" also appears in *Film & History;* in *Rabbit Ears.* Ed. Joel Allegretti. New York: New York Quarterly Press; and *Television Daddy*, by Susanna Rich. Georgetown: Finishing Line Press, 2009.

"The Snake Milker's Daughter" appears in *The Crafty Poet.* Ed. Diane Lockward Nicholasville: Wind, 2013.

"The Trees Are Falling Because They Must" also appears in *Surfing for Jesus* by Susanna Rich. Red Bank: Blast Press, 2017.

"Waldo, Find My Mother in Here" appears in *Beyond the Rift: A North Jersey Literary SocietyAnthology.* Eds. Paul Nash, et al. Providence: The Poet's Press, 2010.

"We're Fringed" also appears in *NJ Poets: Palisades, Parkways & Pinelands.* Brown, Gregg and Emanuel DiPasquale, eds. Cliffwood: Blast Press, 2016.

<143>

ABOUT THIS BOOK

The body type for this book is Franklin Gothic, one of the great classic display faces of the early 20th Century. When this face was designed by Morris Fuller Benton in 1902, the term "Gothic" was used to describe modern-looking sans-serif typefaces, quite contrary to today's conception of "Gothic." Although the face has had many competitors, and faded from view between the two World Wars, its use resurged in the 1940s. Its distinctive letterforms and legibility kept it in type catalogs through the phototypesetting era and well into the digital era. Headlines are in Franklin Gothic Heavy.

The cover design incorporates a detail of the Esterházy Palace at Erdöd, Hungary, and a photograph of a plaster cast of the hand of pianist-composer Franz Liszt. The gates of the Esterházy Palace are shown on the title-page, and graphics extracted from the gate pattern are used as minor section headings.

www.ingramcontent.com/pod-product-compliance
Lightning Source LLC
Chambersburg PA
CBHW022010080426
42733CB00007B/549